n Vineyards of Paris

Geoffrey Finch

ARD AND BENCH
— PUBL

Wine-Producing Vineyards

1 Lycée Albert de Mun, 75007
2 Rue Blanche Fire Station, 75009
3 Clos Bercy, 75012
4 L'Institut Clorivière, 75012
5 Clos des Morillons, 75015
6 La Vigne de Paris-Bagatelle, 75016
7 Hôpital Bretonneau, 75018
8 Clos Montmartre, 75018
9 Jardin de la Treille, 75019
10 Clos Bergerve, 75019
11 Clos des Envierges (Belleville), 75020

Non Wine-Producing Vineyards

12 Parc Joseph Migaret, 75004
13 Le Clos des Arènes (Arènes de Lutèce), 75005
14 Jardin des Plantes, 75005
15 Saint Germain-des-Prés, 75006
16 Jardin Catherine Labouré, 75007
17 Presbytère de Saint Francois Xavier, 75007
18 Bistrot Mélac, 75011
19 Jardin Truillot, 75011
20 Square Léo Ferré, 75012
21 Jardin de Reuilly - Paul Pernin, 75012
22 Le Clos Reuilly, 75012
23 La Commanderie du Clos, 75018

BOIS DE BOULOGNE

16TH

32

9TH

20TH

12TH

BOIS DE VINCENNES

WINE-PRODUCING
VINEYARDS

NON WINE-PRODUCING
VINEYARDS

ISOLATED VINES

The Hidden Vineyards of

Published by Board & Bench I
2055 California St., Suite 2(
San Francisco, CA 94109

Cover and book design: I. Domingo, J
Map design: Julie Rocher
Font: Baskerville
Photos by the author unless otherwis

ISBN 9780932664488
Printed in the USA

i

of man, and joy is the mother of all virtues

 is a series of walks I began hosting some years
ris Wine Walks (www.paris-wine-walks.com). These
cycling) tours have been the ideal marriage of my
vineyards, and my desire to share them with others.
n I am among vines, and seeking out those hidden
of Paris has been a labour of love.

here were vineyards in Paris, but like most people,
f their true extent. Over the past few years, I have
researching these locations, visiting them, and on
emely rare wines they produce. I continue to make
in there are more to make. The parks and gardens
is seem to share my enthusiasm for vines as there
ng up in the parks of the city practically every year.

an more than 2,000 years ago and continues to this
e than 30-million tourists each year, and yet how
that the banks of the Seine, which runs through the
e home to the largest vineyard in the entire world
 planted vines? For the wine enthusiast, beautiful
f Paris's wine-producing past remain hidden within
e vineyards alive and well.

e vineyards that can be found in Paris today, this
t their location, the grape varieties that are planted,
ne producing or not. Although it is intended as a
Paris, their history and enduring presence, it is also
st study but also a very personal one. Biodynamic
tion and burgeoning interest in natural wines has
ny wine world view. The importance of living soils
first experienced working in an organic vineyard,
preciation of natural wine. Enjoying natural wine
ch comes from the Greek 'enthousiasmos', to have
give us joy, strength, and encouragement.

aris is wine. The city grew out of wine, was shaped
y one of the best places on earth to enjoy a glass.

Contents

ould be more obvious? And yet there is a hidden
 living wines that few people ever see. How many
currently almost a dozen wine-producing vineyards
onal dozen non-producing vineyards thriving in
 of the city.
aris is wine and, apart from the spiritual uplift it
ine was also the original economic driver for the
 e 12th century the Seine Valley was renowned in
 s wines were sold throughout the region, bringing

 is book Vin, Vigne et Vignerons (Wine, Vines and
 t "everyone agrees that the quality of the soils and
 are important elements that explain the success of
 is"[1]. The wines were very highly regarded, especially
 eligious orders that were largely responsible for the
 ught quality over quantity. The wine of Suresnes (a
, was appreciated as much as the great Burgundies.
 ch as Pinot de Bourgogne (Pinot Noir) and Gamay
 nteau (another name for Savagnin) for the whites
The popular wines sold as far away as England,

en region Parisienne, Marcel Lachiver, P. 21

Paris was once the largest vineyard area in the

10 wine producing vineyards in Paris.

onal 16 vineyards that don't produce wine.

Viticulture reached its height in the Île-de-France
area and quality around the time of the first empire
when vine acreage exceeded that of Bordeaux and
imagine now that under the historic streets of Par
in the city's soil and that in some neighbourhood
thrive. These vineyards often produced wines com
best of France in both quantity and quality. The vir
in some quarters vestiges still exist) but their preser
names such as the rue Beautreillis, rue du Clos, Pa
le Cour St-Emilion, rue du Clos Feuquières, rue de
Morillons, rue de la Pressoir, rue des Vignes, Cité c
and rue des Vignobles.

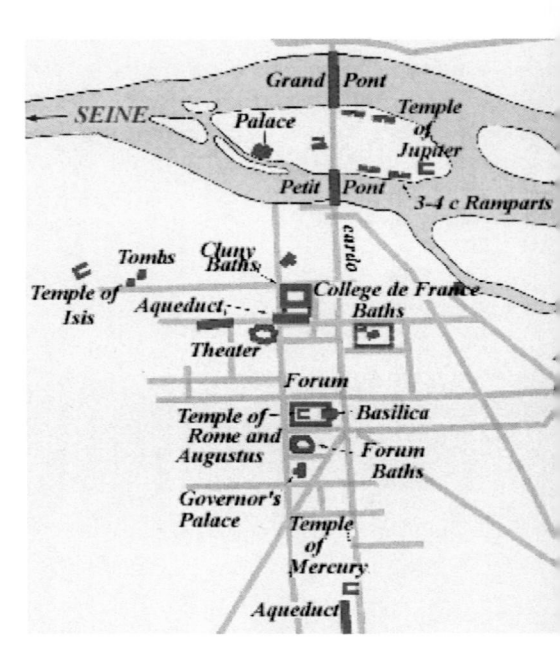

Section of a map of Roman Paris (after Crypte Archéologique 2

s of vine that produces the grapes most commonly
a very tenacious and resistant plant that has been
0 years, its earliest origins for winemaking traced
sus. Vines were present in France in the period of
ntury BC – they are said to have originated with
th of France. It was the Romans we have to thank
tion from the 1st century BC to the beginning of
he 6th century AD. In Roman culture, wine was an
e and even viewed as a necessity. In contrast to the
here wine was pretty much limited to the clergy and
s mostly drank cider, ale or perry), wine in Roman
nd drunk by nobles, women, children, and slaves
nd more particularly with the Romans, it was mixed
ably less alcoholic than the wines we have today.

re grew, so did the vine. To supply armies with
eyards were planted wherever Roman garrisons
tlements established – as far north as England.
s had a history of wine making were given the
ting these vineyards and making the wine. France
nd and climate for growing grapes. Though there
ietals imported from Italy, it is thought that most of
us varietals and hence the ancestors of the grapes
oday.

as significant, providing the foundation for the vast
at is France today. Starting in the southern regions
doc and the Southern Rhône, where the wines were
character to those one might have found in Italy
made with sun-drenched, fully mature grapes) the
l north establishing vineyards along the Garonne
hors, Gaillac, Bergerac), which were identified
vere shipped from there, and on to the areas of
he Loire, Burgundy and the Jura, the Île-de-France,
.

t in the 6th century AD, the clergy took over the
as lands were owned either by the church or by
The clergy worked the vines for the glory of God,

devoting their lives to the church to make 'the b
finance the economy of daily life and to build ten
these institutions amassed extraordinary wealth ir
belonging to the aristocracy and the king were w
derived scant reward in return.

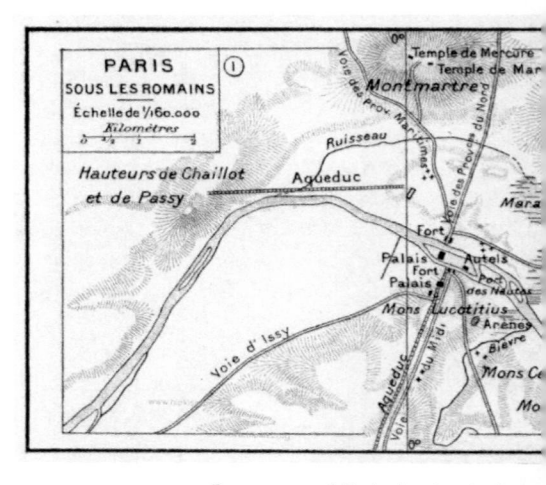

Roman map of Paris showing the Arena,

Did you know...

🍇 The first grape vines in France were planted in
settlers in the 6th century BC.

🍇 The Romans are mostly responsible for the sp
around Paris.

🍇 Wine has been produced in Paris for over 20 c

🍇 The wines of Bordeaux were originally from
Bergerac.

🍇 After the Romans, the church expanded viney
quantities of wine.

and Sales

f Gothic architecture, which dates from the 12th
nd like a rather fanciful statement, but it was the
and the wealth garnered from the sale of wine that
onditions for Gothic architecture to flourish. Gothic
 and developed in the Paris basin, which stretches
ns to Chartres and east to west from Senlis to Sens.
m the sale of wine abroad brought enormous riches
stocracy. Wealth, architectural skill, a ready labour
naterials for building made it possible for the great
nce to be built. Most of these are centred in and
such as cathedrals in Amiens, Bourges, Chartres,
 de Paris, the Sainte Chapelle, the Abbey church
a few.

ne quantities of wine that flowed through Paris were
d that per-capita wine production in France was
ating a cash surplus that afforded a deeply religious
ilding to the glory of God. The best vineyards at
the areas where the Gothic style was created and

Medieval Grape Harvest

flourished. It can then be said that wine is the single n
factor in the cultural and spiritual growth of the ti

Notre .

Did you know…

🍇 The wines of the Middle Ages were only 7°,
mixed with water.

🍇 The wines of the Paris region were renowned
the Middle Ages.

🍇 Gothic architecture originated in the Seine V

🍇 The sale of wine generated great wealth, pro
create Gothic Architecture.

l area in France, the vines of the Île-de-France went
he 19th century, to the point of practically being
here and there around Paris have sustained the
tness but are known only to an informed coterie of
and are completely ignored by the general public.

tly due to urbanisation as the wealth generated
ich' wines grew (in the Middle Ages, 'France' was
ce), with housing and industry replacing vineyards.
rotecting agricultural lands from construction and
s not new and has for centuries been the source of
nce between those we would today call ecologists
to as developers.

ontributed to this decline was a drop in quality.
Ages, peasants were deprived of wine and drank
'pomace', a drink made of water filtered through
is often contaminated. From the 17th century,
f the population began drinking wine, quantity
ility in the Île-de-France, carrying on through to
volution in the late 18th century. The traditional
ie clergy– switched to wines from Burgundy and
on networks developed, particularly the railroad.
son for the collapse in the reputation of 'French'
ise in the reputations of Burgundy and Bordeaux.

iere are 200 vineyards in and around Paris.

the steam engine that caused the phylloxera

ee weeks to cross the Atlantic and steamships

e victims of their own success, driving urban
g the vineyards.

The phylloxera blight of the mid-19th century
most vineyard areas of the Île-de-France as they
the cheaper wines arriving from the southern regi
the Languedoc Roussillon, and so were never rep

But there is a renaissance in progress. In recent ye
area of vines planted in the Paris region has tripled a
awarded with the distinction of its own IGP label
protégée or protected designation of origin). Today
Île-de-France has around twenty professional vineya
planted or being planted. Patrice Bersac, the pres
Vignerons d'Ile-de-France (SYVIF - Syndicate of Île
says "we plan to reach 300 ha within two years. S
from Seine-et-Marne, are planning to diversify and
into their activities".

Parisians have been drinking their own wine for
quantity, the quality and the range has varied from
recent trend is very positive. There has been renew
consumption. More 'cavistes' (wine shops) have op
in Paris than have ever been open before. And wi
English in their modern form (where what you fi
to rise to the level of the wine in your glass), have
the wines so good, it's difficult not to stumble upo

This was not always the case, as up until quite
be a sociological division between the good and
wines were served in almost every café, bistro, r
There were the happy few who could afford ac
then there was everyone else. The recognition of
been forgotten with an appalling range of undri
everywhere with not the slightest protestation.

What changed? There have been several
contributed to this renaissance. As new world
greater attention along with more objective cr
evidenced by a burgeoning number of wine
bloggers who have challenged the status quo.
makers motivated by quality rather than by quar
of biodynamic and organic farming methods,
becoming the norm. Biodynamic farming, enti

instream. Large holdings taken over by a younger
educed to what can be properly managed by one
es), minimising financial pressures and freeing the
aints imposed by industrial methods.

ave been taken by those challenging the dictates
ons d'Origine Contrôlée) to plant varietals that
appellation', thereby sacrificing the right to the
not having the AOC designation meant a drop in
s losing its credibility as being a mark of quality,
these innovators are making better wines without
go so far as to abjure it entirely, buying only wines
on (Vin de France). Driven by a passion for quality
g the 'terroir' to express itself rather than imposing
the wine—wine growers who no longer value the
oughout the country, generally selling their wines
s.

peared in France in the 1930s as a guarantee of
ically, of quality, has been steadily losing its sheen
is are simple. Wines produced from soils that are
essively lose their microbial life, which is the very
sequently, these industrial or 'conventional' wines
press their terroir, which is the most fundamental
tity.

ing naturally (organically and biodynamically)
dictates of the AOC who have returned to a true
vitalising soils, have often been eliminated from the
termined by peer review. Conventional producers,
e AOC, find these natural wines 'atypical' and so
pellation. Which is of course another mark against
ch exclusions, quite logically, as the world turned
producing wines that are a true representation of
e the best expressions of an AOC and not wines
with dubious additives because their grapes have
ing been produced in dead soils.
were intended to precisely delimit the appellation
nd to fraud and counterfeiting. Soon they were
o regulations concerning grape varieties, yields,
al practices. These regulations were in principle

inspired by the 'local, loyal, and constant practices
and supposed to guarantee the 'typicity' of the win
that the greatest fraud are 'conventional' wines, wh
AOC, because they no longer express terroir or t'
d'Origine Contrôlée was created by a decree-law
wines and eaux-de-vie. The body responsible for the
and control, the INAO (originally the Institut N.
d'Origine, now the Institut National de l'Origin
created in the same year.

In 2009 the AOP, the European equivalent of th
though the term 'AOC' persists in France. Th
specifications brought about by the changeover to AC
Protégée or PDO - Protected Designations of Ori
life into quality. While the designation is a guara
not necessarily a guarantee of quality. The opport
specifications applicable to these standards is also
the level of requirements.

Did you know...

🍇 The AOC was created to protect consumers

🍇 Before 'mise en bouteille au château' or dom
shipped in barrels to their destinations and unscr
would often mix inferior wine with those of grea

🍇 The Paris region lost its status as a wine produ
wines produced in the Île-de-France from being

🍇 In 2016 the Paris region officially regained it
producer and there are now approximately thirt
producing wine for sale.

🍇 Paris has been identified as a wine producing
to being part of the IGP (Indication Géographic
(Denomination Géographique Complémentaire

ines

this natural resistance is natural wine. Of course,
such wine have chosen to plant varietals other than
OC. Their resistance to the AOC takes the form
of making little or no attempt at being accepted by
e 'inferior' denomination of VDF (Vin de France).
vines that are out of the ordinary, affirming their
choice in varietal selection, blends, and vinification
of proposing real wines that fully express their terroir.

ement has its origins in the region of Beaujolais in
auvet and Jacques Neauport, two oenologists who
nes with fewer additives, and again in Beaujolais in
of four' of Marcel Lapierre, Jean Foillard, Charly
on. However, it is only in the past few years that
strong enough to practically eclipse conventional
y identified as 'natural' are wines with no additional
also be grown organically or biodynamically and
yeasts. Apart from no additional sulphur, there are
wine making process – and filtration and fining are
ist grapes, nothing else.

ents among enthusiasts about the definition of
e that it is acceptable to add sulphur before bottling,
ficantly under those of conventional wines. Others
ze. But all agree that no chemicals are permitted in
es in the wine making, and that fermentation must
ts and little or no sulphur. A simple and concise
ded, nothing taken away'.

an be the most sublime expressions of terroir, are
barnyard smells and high levels of volatile acidity.
can offer the most astonishing purity and depth,
harmony of tastes, opening slowly and rising to
liscover through tasting them. Paris has become the
to the great joy of most oenophiles, as those days
the city's 'bars à vins' and cafés (which can sadly
arters of the city) have happily been replaced with
natural living wines with creative names and even
e thing that is certain is that natural wines will not

poison you or leave you with the unpleasant after
the following day after drinking conventional wine

Which brings us back to Paris and the history o
the Middle Ages were everywhere and a staple of da
Though they were extensive, they were never very l
a few ares (100 square metres) and managed by a si
no pesticides, fungicides, insecticides or herbicide
did not exist, and these chemicals had not yet bec
weren't on soils that wouldn't support other crops
example), vines were often planted among grain
dotted with fruit trees creating balanced ecosyster
for beneficial insects and the biodiversity needed
soils. Practices that are again being embraced by
wine growers.

Though it is difficult now to determine exactly
Paris were, the fact that they were so extensive, en
afar, and consumed in very large quantities would
very much appreciated. In some respects, one mi
return to natural farming and wine-making practi
to the simple, yet highly productive practices of n

The large abbeys of Saint-Germain-des-Prés
Dame de Paris possessed extensive vineyards situa
well as in over 130 other communes. The daily life
was intimately associated with wine and cultiva
still is) labour intensive work that kept many a sou
revenue as well as an antidote to the hardships of

The great vineyards of Paris and the Paris
centuries, right up until the 19th century. As an inte
and culture and as a source of revenue for religious
were planted everywhere they could be, with at ti
so more vines could be planted. It cannot be deni
like the Aquitaine plateau, is a magnificent viticu
land of wine'. But as the prosperity that was gene
these wines grew, so did urbanisation, gradually
houses and buildings. The wines of Paris were vic
driving urban expansion and so uprooting the vi

ural wine made by Laurent Lebled

g started in Beaujolais in the 1930s and then was
0s.

eed nothing more than grapes.

' built in 1662 (where Jussieu University and
 are today) was the largest wine storage facility
ive until 1954.

n of vine plants in the world (nearly 2,000
 be in the south-west corner of the Luxembourg

re is the largest vineyard in Paris and the vines
Germain-des-Prés is the smallest.

Legacy of the Vine

s sunlight, held together by water
— *Galileo*

aris Today

ned for its vineyards and the extraordinary diversity
it might seem normal to find vines in its capital.
ven realize they are there. They are discreet and
the conscious minds of people who pass them by,
:d, yet rooted in soils that have seen centuries of
almost magical link through to this historical past
gour an emblem of nature's power, muted though
awling urban landscape.

– Wine-producing Vineyards

l wine-producing vineyards in the city along
o that evoke the spirit of Dionysus (without wine
ply decorative, each one an eloquent reminder
al past. The best known is the Clos Montmartre as
y year with a three-day village-like celebration that
iprised of locals and tourists who often happen
e.

e-producing vineyards cultivated by the city include
lissement, the Clos des Morillons in the 15th, the
/illette) and the Clos Bergeyre in the 19th and the
20th. Along with these city owned and operated
'independent' vineyards: the Albert de Mun high
offers a course in sommellerie), the fire station on
th, the Institut Clorivière in the 12th (a wine and
: de Paris Bagatelle in the 16th and the Hôpital
Though it is the intention of the newly planted
de Lutèce to produce wine, it will be several years
: 'taken' and rooted sufficiently to produce grapes
tion.

ed 'Winerie Parisienne' has built a winery on the 1st
They began in 2015 by making wines from selected
ie country but in 2017 planted 10 hectares of vines
Davron to the west of Paris. The varietals are Pinot
reds and Chardonnay, Chenin and Sauvignon for
wines are made from grapes "coming from great

French terroirs and the assemblages are modern
the best French terroirs".

The Winerie Parisienne is not alone in setting u
'Les Vignerons Parisiens' on the rue Turbigo in
have been vinifying a range of wines from the Côt
using grapes that have, for the most part, been cu
There is therefore no real connection here with t
the Île-de-France, other than the fact that the gr
are vinified in the city.

Grapes from Albert de Mun

(Not open to the public)

is wine taught in high school? That it is possible
er in a high school might seem a radical idea to
here the consumption of alcohol is discouraged
t in France, an appreciation for wine is part of a
ns centuries and extends over the entire country.

14 the 370 students of the Albert de Mun High
0 vines, primarily in the courtyard of their school
approach, the school's intention being that all the
the 12 students in the sommelier class, be aware
a vineyard until the wine is bottled.

king grapes at Lycée Albert de Mun

Twelve Piwi grape varieties (an abbreviation fc
Rebsorten' or fungus-resistant grape varieties) from (
were planted, since they are relatively low maintena
the vine's vegetative cycles from theory to practic
winemaking had already taken place at the schoc
brought in to make a dry white wine. Like the Instit
the Albert de Mun high school thus has its own vin
with a hands-on approach to viticulture and vinifi

Now that the school has its own vineyard, it has
wine, the first vintage having been made in 2018.

Making wine at the Lycée Albert

tion
▸

ue Blanche, with its seventeen long trellised vines
elas, dating from 1929, celebrates harvest every
d'ornement' – ornamental wine, or a wine that is
than serious wine making – that the fire station's
drinkable' if you value your health. Nevertheless,
of 'Château Blanche' have been made each year
ven away to the firemen and their families and to
notables living in the quarter. Tradition has it that
een married in the year get to stomp the grapes
abaret dancers from the nearby Moulin Rouge. A
d to add prestige and the folklore of rural harvest
sforms the neighbourhood into a village bacchanal.

Clos Bercy
Access from 1 rue Joseph Kessel, 75012

The vineyard of the Parc de Bercy is a meagre
once the location of the biggest wine storage facili
682m² of vines of Sauvignon and Chardonnay gr
wine grapes were planted in the 'Yitzak Rabin' g
Park, which produce a light, pleasantly fruity wir
two vineyards here. One that looks like the rows
anywhere in any wine region of the world, and t
with vines tangling themselves along trellises a
the ground. Nearby, close to the parapet by the C
underground 'chai' or wine cellar that is used to vir
each year from Bercy, Bergeyre, and Belleville.

The history of the wine storage facility of Ber
history of the Halle aux Vins, which was located
where Jussieu University and the World Arab In
Established in 1662 and expanded in 1808, the
wine storage facility for Paris until the mid-1800's.
the population tripled, as did wine consumption,
covering 14 hectares of land (about 35 acres) prov

458. PARIS. — Entrepôts de Bercy Rue de Bloye.

rge shipments of barrels from all over France via
ing to the Seine (the Canal de Bourgogne connecting
ls into the Seine and the Canal Latéral à la Loire
the Rhône and the eastern Loire also feeding into
h coastal shipments to the Seine from Bordeaux,
and the Western Loire, contributed to a surge in
g from a million hectolitres at the beginning of the
by 1865.

facility was needed and Bercy was chosen. At the
valls of the city, its vineyards and taverns therefore
hais' (cellars) were built along alleys named after the
le Bordeaux, rue de Champagne, rue de Meursault,
). Storage was augmented further to accommodate
Midi (Provence, Languedoc Roussillon…) via the
hectares (about 100 acres) were dedicated to the
ed Paris until the 1960s. Meanwhile, the Halle aux
de storage for wines on the left bank up until the
wine, was a depot for spirits.

varehouses was limited to the depot workers, wine
nts, though there was a passenger train track that
a to and from the Gare de Lyon. Wine bars, taverns
air cafés located along the banks of the Seine) had
y since the early 18th century because the wine was
aris. In the 19th century, it became the 'in place' to
places like the Rocher de Cancale, the Marronniers

and the Soleil d'Or, drawn not only by the wine
included frequent fireworks displays and fairgrou

When much of the area was being redeveloped
of Bercy was to reveal itself as ancient pirogues, fl.
were found along with an archery bow made of yew
to the 5th millennium BC, making it one of the old

Regrettably, the vast storage areas and dock.
have either been demolished or reduced to a con
single museum or reference to the vine. Today's '
attempt to mimic Covent Garden in London and
animated this historic area of Paris has been forgo
food restaurants, tourist bars, and commercial win
whatsoever to what was once known as 'happy Be

t, 75012 (Not open to the public)

pirits Institute is located a few steps from Place de la
e Napoléon Foundation. It is only appropriate that
. Planted to 100-vines that are used for educational
ilso has a winery, and a professional tasting room
ary 2017.

resident of the SYVIF (Syndic des Vignerons en
e instructor here. Every year the students make a
planted in the back of the institute, which is an
ent varietals. According to Bersac, the wine is not
ght be, especially given the differences in ripeness
pen earlier than others. But there have been years
ity of some of the grapes makes up for the over-
ipes, creating a balance that can be quite pleasant.

institute is to train professionals in the sector in
he courses ranging from 3 hours to several days.
& Spirits', accredited centre of the WSET school
e trains apprentices and students so that they can
1, 2 and 3 certification.

Clos des Morillons
50 Rue des Morillons, 75015

The Clos des Morillons is in the Parc Georges
once hosted the Vaugirard slaughterhouses. In th
conducted a poll that determined most residents
slaughterhouses to be replaced by a park. A group o
the idea of planting vines as a homage to the vin
plateau that had been generously planted to vines
debate ensued between a Norman senator and a o
the 15th. The former wanted to plant apple trees
notorious 'cider over wine' battle followed, with the

The slaughterhouses were demolished, and constru
park began. Only the two pavilions at the entrance t
which was also the site of the 'criée' or auction whe
remain of the historic buildings. In 1982, the choi
vines was left to the mayor and the director of the I
A gentle, south-facing slope was chosen, the soil cl
700 vines of Pinot Noir and a few Chasselas were
in March 1983, over a surface of 1200 square me

The first harvest took place in 1985 and bro
inhabitants, the mayor and the Commanderie of the
480 kilos were picked, which were then vinified i

nt for this includes two 600 litre vats, a press and
els. Following the classic phases of vinification, the
barrels for 3 to 4 months before being bottled (on
les). Half of this is given as gifts to locally elected
ld at auction for local charities.

a Champagne coloured, 'Hollandaise' style, with
. The vineyard itself is little known outside of its
od. In the past, this was intentional as the mayor
scouraging it from becoming an object for tourism.
1 to keep it as a witness of the past and an occasion
her around 'their' vines as a symbol of life, gaiety
s.

es Morillons terrace

La Vigne de Paris-Bagatelle
10 Route du Champ d'Entraînement, 75016 (

Situated at the edge of the Bois de Boulogne, near
La Défense, the domain de La Vigne de Paris-Ba
vines in the private garden of a mansion built in
de Kapurthalan. The structure has been entirely
owner, comtesse Christian d'Andlau-Hombourg.
lush green park and the vines are planted right ne
of grass. The setting is beautiful and extraordinar
from the urban world around it is easy to forget o

A blend of Pinot Noir and Pinot Blanc, the gr
premises in the domain's own winery. Producing bet
a year, the eponymous Sparkling Comte et Comte
Hombourg is a sparkling wine, made using the 'm
is the only sparkling wine vinified in Paris and the
high environmental quality zone (ISO 14001) prac
and is moving towards biodynamics.

s events, private receptions and wine courses and
ellar and taste this rare wine by appointment with
irg, the cellar master. The family also has a vineyard
nbine a tasting of the wine of the Bagatelle with

ducing sparkling wine

Hôpital Bretonneau
23 Rue Joseph de Maistre, 75018 (Limited ac

The geriatric Bretonneau Hospital at 23 Rue Joseph
has a hidden vineyard of 125 vines of Malbec, pla
grape most associated in France with Cahors. Alth
associated with Paris, being rather thick skinned
lot of sun to ripen, Malbec was chosen because the
has ties with the Cahors region. Its selection is thus
world vineyards that are often planted with variet
correspond to the climate.

Climate change might be an ally here though
summers are any indication of this trend, they
ripening in the future. The wine that is produced
wine producing vineyards, can be sampled once a
la Vigne'. All the hospital's personnel, along wit
participate in the harvest, directed by Fabrice Du
appropriately, is from Vire-sur-Lot (Cahors). The wi
'on the property' right in the hospital in the cella
especially for it.

Viney

(Access by reservation only)

10 doesn't know the 'Clos Montmartre', the most
muros vineyards. The Clos Montmartre epitomises
butes greatly to giving one the impression of being
ing crowds of the city. This sense of being in the
nded vines covering the gentle slope of the 'clos'
talgia for the old Montmartre, glimpses of which
nt today.

homage to the vine, the 'mount's' vinous history
e. The hilltop was already a place of worship and
Christian times, and the columns of the old church
ond oldest church in Paris after Saint-Germain-
n a temple dedicated to Bacchus. The Emperors
Julien vaunted its wines and were followed by the
eginning of the 12th century, Adelaide de Savoie,
ontmartre Abbey, launched a campaign to extend

ito: Lei Saito)

the abbey's vineyards, which were for a long whi
revenue. The wine produced there was called 'Sa
meaning 'sack of lees', otherwise known as Clare

There were six 'clos' of Montmartre planted
is just to the left of the Eglise Saint Pierre; Haute
of Sacre Coeur are now; and below it to the left, cu
Saint Pierre, was the Bas Coteau. Right below the
the rue d'Orsel was Rochefoucauld. The vineyar
Sacre Coeur stands was called 'Clos de l'Eglise'. /
place Jean-Baptiste Clement was 'Bel Air'. There
of the Moulin du Vin along the Allée des Brouilla

Most of these vineyards were planted by the
Montmartre. Wine was not just something needed fo
drink, it was used medicinally and for cooking, a
that could provide income.

Vines prospered here until the Revolution in
vineyard cultivation difficult, despite the wines her
Goutte d'Or) having attained notoriety as one of
of a world classification after *Malvoisie and Cyp

tre

as Malvasia is in Italy. A wide range of often unrelated varieties
most are light-berried and make full-bodied, aromatic white
nonly encountered, in the Loire, Savoie and Switzerland, as a
Languedoc's Bourboulenc and Maccabéo, Roussillon's Tourbat
all been called Malvoisie in their time, however. (Vines, Grapes

e convention of Saint Cloud and the surrender of
mander, the Duke of Wellington, the 'butte' was
who laid many of the vineyards to waste (which
s with their traditional thirst for the grape). Later,
of the slopes began and one-by-one the vineyards
co-Prussion war of 1870 then destroyed the few

e vine in Montmartre got under way in 1933. The
ions took possession of the land where the current
a group of Montmartrois, with the painter Poulbot
in preventing a 5-story apartment building from

being built there. The mayor of Thomery (a can
planted the first vine from the celebrated Dom
December 1933. The first harvest in 1935 was a
of the Chamber of Deputies, Edouard Herriot,
period such as Mistinguett and Fernandel as well as
having been planted only two years earlier, the vir
anything worth harvesting, which lead to a potent
But again, the vineyards of Thomery and elsewl
and donated grapes so that Montmartre could have
grapes were pressed in the Place du Tertre and the

The 2,500 vines planted were a confusion of ne
(Pinot Blanc, Muscat Blanc, Morgon, Sauvignon, C
Villard, among others), which led to uneven ripen
for harvest. These have now been replaced and
70% Gamay, 10% Pinot Noir and 20% of the or
Sauvignon, Chasselas, Seyve-Villard, etc.). The v
under trees produce very little and the fact that t
facing doesn't help.

has taken place in the Mairie (town hall) of the 18th
986, which was a good year, more than a tonne of
ucing between 600 and 700 litres of wine; whereas
ar, produced only 300 litres. On average, between
produced annually of a rosé with 7° to 9° alcohol
ccording to the Montmartrois winemakers, it is a
ugh', 'lively' and 'drinkable'. The wine produced
y red and about 11° to 12° alcohol, is not without
ction of being the only wine produced by the city
mercially (35€ for a 50 cl bottle − available in the
de Montmartre, or contact the 'Comité des Fêtes
the 18th arrondissement of Paris).

are sold at auction, often attaining prices that well
e, but their rarity and novelty make them interesting
rvest festivities take place every year, generally on
tober, and are attended by various 'confréries' in
s. The Godfather and Godmother of the vine are
the world of show business, who accompany the
mayor of the arrondissement, and together they
e of the grapes. Depending on the maturity of the
kes place either before or after the harvest festivities.

vineyard has been part of Paris' heritage for some
me prestige as any of its monuments. But unlike
inspire intellectual or aesthetic appreciation, the
lively, simple, village festivity. Thanks of course to
you prefer).

Jardin de la Treille
Parc de La Villette, 75019

The La Villette park in the north of Paris is the h
but perhaps the least well known is the Jardin de
produced until 2010. These vines, planted at the c
cultivated on high, are more than 30 years old. It v
Agnès and Philippe Chariol, who produce a granc
(Gironde), that this vineyard was planted.

The Chasselas vine stocks, planted in 1988, a
trellis forming a ceiling in this shaded garden. T
the 90 small fountains that run down the stepped
corner of plant paradise. Seven bronze sculpture
Jean-Max Albert, dominate this idyllic setting, remir
association the vine has with the arts. In the fall, th
to make the 'vin de la treille'.

The first harvest was in 2009 and the wine de
"very young, very green, but very nice, to pair with
time, only 280 bottles were produced, including 2
not much, and you won't find it in any cellar near y
insider wine is reserved for journalists, and especia
La Villette, the only ones who can bring a bottle h
it, it will be for a cause of general interest," says
partnerships and patronage at the Parc and Grande
was a second vintage in 2010, but since then there

nnois, 75019
r during 'La Fête de la Vigne')

ace amidst the noise and bustle of Paris is so well
ns know of its existence. Only one road leads into
side very close to the Butte de Chaumont, a larger
ars are practically non-existent.

ts today on the Butte Bergeyre was planted in 1995
of a municipal gardener. Oriented west and very
f the terraced vineyards of Hermitage, Alsace or
e are 230 vines of Chardonnay, Muscat and Pinot
ach year, yielding between 150-200 kilos of grapes.
cellars at Bercy (which also vinifies the grapes of
roducing about 60 litres of wine each year. The

los Bergeyre

grapes are crushed together to create a pale rosé w
from year to year, and which is very light but insp

Beginning in the 13th century, the slopes o
Ménilmontant were a vast territory of gypsum
ingredient in 'plaster of Paris'), which eventually c
Bergeyre. There were already a few vines on the slop
pastureland reserved for cattle, and from the 16th
also constructed. A total of six were built on this t
own name: 'Grand', 'Tour de Chaumont', 'la Caros
and 'Folie'. They were demolished in 1778 and le

Work on the neighbouring Butte de Chaumont
spared the Butte Bergeyre, which remained in its v
more years. Construction of the Rothschild Ho
1905 as part of an urbanisation project, and in 1
'Les Folles Buttes' was built on the other side of the
that a music hall and an outdoor cinema were soo

Later, tennis courts and a stadium were built on t
had remained free of houses, home only to cows

anted to build a rugby pitch and so work began in
rt and considerable expense, the stadium, which
0 people, was completed in 1918 and was named in
re, a rugby player who was killed in action in 1914.
osted the Olympic Games, the Bergeyre stadium
f spectacles and attractions featuring personalities
lie Chaplin and Maurice Chevalier. Maintenance
e work of shoring up the foundations and so it was
oper in 1925.
d into lots and sold in 1928, all the single dwelling
ely. But the land that had once housed 'Les Folles
d and so became a playground for children and
um seekers and those running from the law. The
were taken over by artists and the affluent, drawn
y of life and the bucolic sensibility of the place.

Clos des Envièrges (Belleville)
Junction of rue Piat, rue des Envierges, rue ⦗
(Open only once a year during 'La Fête de la ⦘

Belleville was celebrated for its wines from the Mi⦗
of its vineyards carried on until the 1950s, although
As a 'quartier populaire', or working-class neighbo⦗
and vineyards were essential for sustaining a su⦘
though the quality of the wines declined as land a⦗
scarcer. Among the last sectors of Paris to become
come under municipal jurisdiction until 1860 and
the last areas of the city to have working vineyard⦗
was outside the walls of Paris, so the wines were u⦗
to loosen up, dance, and drink 'guinguet', a you⦗
eventually gave its name to the guinguettes, or wi⦗

The 'clos' or enclosed vineyards maintained b⦗
'plateau de Savies', currently Belleville and produce⦗

Gr⦘

epers and tavern-keepers settled in the village and
oundant amount of mediocre wine that persisted
verns and guinguettes competed for places there
a century.

, the celebrated tavern of the publican Ramponneau,
ved a young, slightly effervescent wine made from
led 'Piquette'. Over time this use has changed,
s to a drink made from pomace and water and is
to a bad wine (the French equivalent of 'plonk').

es vineyard

In the Middle Ages, numerous religious com
of land on the hill. They cleared fields, planted
numerous springs. At the time, there was a water sh
of Paris, which had been supplied from the platea
2nd century but damaged during the Great Invasior
in the 9th century. Water then came from the Sei
at the time. But drawing water from the river was
since the Seine was often far away and in high den
since the 12th century had been damaged becau
not very efficient. As of the 12th century, Bellevil
the Eastern side of the city, with religious orders
financing the construction of aqueducts.

The opening of a gypsum quarry in the 1!
population of seasonal workers (often stonemason:
Haussmann's construction projects during the wint
the summer to tend their fields. The area was dee
didn't improve with the closing of the quarry.

In the 19th century, the cottages which at the
of the steps leading up to the present-day park gav
like that of Montmartre. They belonged to Julien
important landowners of the hill of Belleville, a
alongside the park now bears his name. At this tir
organized each year on the hill for Mardi Gras.
Mardi Gras carnival, all of Paris came en masse to
la Courtille', one of the three major Mardi Gras
the cheap restaurants that lined the rue de Bellevil
Hardi' (The Hardy Rooster) and 'La Carotte Filan
Carrot) were well known for the drinking binges o

At the end of the 20th century, the cottages of
to more modern buildings and the Parc de Belle
vineyards disappeared and now all that remains is a s
in 1992 to Pinot Meunier vines from Champagne
from Burgundy, a modest reminder of the area's v
the distinction of possibly being the only vineyard
soil that has always been planted to vines (the new
Arènes de Lutèce might also claim this distinction).
Clos Bergeyre and Bercy, it too is vinified in the 'ch
very pleasant, slightly rosé coloured wine. And lik
only be tasted once a year during the 'Fête de la
takes place in the first week of October.

Montmartre

in general) no wines

enaissance happening in Paris, reflected in the
and biodynamic wine shops, professional wine
natural wine bars. The vine itself continues to
ape with new plantings springing up every year.
s, two major plantings have appeared, the most
es de Lutèce in the 5th and the Jardin Truillot in
he wine producing sites within the city, there are
h vines and (mainly) no wine. This is not because
of producing wine, but simply because there are
ify the effort, or the will to do so, and the facilities
g.

ailed descriptions of the main non-wine producing
nber of ornamental, ecological or experimental
ind in various quarters of the city, or single vines
al metres in length. They are listed in the order of
inning with the 4th and moving up:

aret
004

discover this modern-day vineyard in the Marais
ns marsh or swampland and so it might be natural
ever any vineyards planted in this area of the city,
in boggy, wet soil. This was not always the case.
itself began in the 10th century, undertaken by
ated to extend the land they could use for farming
whose extensive palace, the Hôtel Saint Pol built
quite close by near the banks of the Seine and had
autreillis (beautiful trellises) is also an indication
within the palace. Located to the southwest of the
the 4th arrondissement of Paris, the residence's
he quai des Célestins to the rue Saint-Antoine and
to the rue du Petit-Musc.

k on the Hôtel Saint-Pol in 1361. From then until
improve and develop it by acquiring additional
he construction of new buildings. The king, who
lential odours of Paris (at the time a rather small

Marais vines and bench

area of the city that included the islands and par
Bank) and the problems they caused his health,
outside the medieval city. He valued the residence fo
environment, which he claimed had helped him a
importantly recover good health.

The Hôtel Saint-Pol was not a single building
important dwellings making up the royal residen
king, one for the queen, one for their children. All
and entertainments given by the king, and rooms fo
the residence luxuriously decorated according to
featured precious woods, paintings, and goldworl
with hangings embroidered with pearls, and book
furniture along with golden ornaments. Two ch
residence, one for the king, the other for his conso
The hôtel included a remarkable collection of prec
enjoyed assembling, including those of his father
been a great lover of books. This collection allow

would later become the 'Bibliothèque Nationale
ional library in Paris. Within his own residence,
)m for the 'Conseil du Roi' where affairs of state

Parc Joseph Mignaret is emblematic of a much
ese young vines, planted in the 2010s, are more
ve (no wine is made from them), they provide us
ltural history of the Marais and medieval Paris.
ave here are Chasselas Doré and Muscat, neither
'noble' varieties, though Chasselas is possibly one
varieties. According to British wine writer Jancis
d leaves bear a strong resemblance to those painted
l grounds at Luxor in Egypt. Chasselas flourished
nebleau (specifically Thomery) producing popular
royal court. The Muscat family of grapes produce
like ripe table grapes. And given how heady and
)se wines can be, they rarely figure among the most
:ountry.

Vestige of one of the Philippe Auguste towers

The park is named after Joseph Mignaret, a direc
of the nearby elementary school, Les Hospitaliers Sa
who saved many Jewish children from extermination
in 2007 and completed in 2014, the park brings tog
of the mansions that surround it, which are the H
the Maison de l'Europe de Paris) the Hôtel Barbès
The garden is therefore divided into different sect

The first section, behind the Hôtel Albrecht has t
of one of the 77 towers of Philippe August's fortif
at the end of the 12th century and surrounded wha
restored in 2014, it is in relatively poor shape and
history was attached to the Hôtel Albrecht and se
room and a chapel. This section also has trees culti
a wall and a community garden with a fine range

The middle section, behind the Hôtel Barbès, i
as a pathway between the 3 sections. There is a s
side and a chestnut tree on the other.

The third section, the space behind the Hôtel d
grassy area with birch trees and Provençal suga
ceanothus (lilac) shrubs, Mexican orange, dogwood
and feather or spear grasses. In the background is
that is 35 metres tall that belonged to the 'Société d
down the clippings, filings and sweepings from me
gold and silver.

rènes de Lutéce)
Or from the rue des Arènes or the rue de

es again! This most ancient of Parisian historical
und the year 50. Its Roman arena, unearthed and
century during construction of the Place Monge
tion of a medieval vineyard, first cited in the 7th
ng banks of the arena, once occupied with seating
imply covered in grass, offer the perfect pitch for
these slopes were planted to vines, making them
to the vineyards of Paris.

e been planted are disease resistant hybrids called
oreal' developed by the INRA (Institut national de
e). The first two are red grapes. Artaban is planted
c on the South and Floreal on the Southwest slope.
of a neighbourhood association (aptly called the
ention is for this vineyard to serve as an historical
to the quarter's rich viticultural past. It is unclear

yet whether the vineyard will produce wine or no
intention if it proves feasible.

When Lutèce was sacked during the barbarian
some of the structure's stonework was carted o
defences around the Île de la Cité. Subsequently, t
a cemetery, and then it was filled in completely fo
of the Philippe Auguste wall (ca. 1210). Over tin
metres of earth and forgotten for 12 centuries.

The Abbaye Saint Victor, which occupied the
Jardin des Plantes, the campus of Jussieu University
there (Cuvier, Guy de la Brosse, Linné), was, along
Germain-des-Prés and Notre Dame de Paris, endo
land holdings, planted mostly to vines. Saint Victo
of the vines variously referred to as 'les Arènes de S
des Arènes'. Etienne Lafourcade in Paris Pays du V
to the vineyards of Les Arènes, the first dating fro

The author pruning vines in the Clos des Arenes

the vineyard is in the Jardin Écologique)

e banks of the Seine and what is now the 5th
picentre of Roman Paris. The baths of Cluny and
rue Monge are among the vestiges of this period.
eyards attached to the Abbeys of Notre Dame de
1-des-Prés flourished all along the left bank. The
ève, upon which now sits the Pantheon, formed a
to 'clos' or enclosures, with streets still bearing their
los Garlande...).

is the 2nd oldest park in Europe – after the Botanical
– and is classed as an historical monument. The
he public for almost 400 years, housing tremendous
colours and perfumes, and is a source of knowledge
vation. Though shaped by scientists and gardeners,
ture of the only botanical garden in the capital has
ed by kings, queens, damsels, dandies, great ladies,
lovers, and an ever-increasing number of joggers.

Created in the 17th century (1626), upon the in
Heroard and Guy de la Brosse, the Jardin des Plan
to species with medicinal and therapeutic virtue
became a research centre and museum, under the
Louis Leclerc, comte de Buffon. After the Revolution
development. The many buildings of the garde
monuments, were built during this exceptional p
Mineralogy Gallery, the Great Gallery of Evolution
The history of the park is vast and its scientific leg
a sense of this expanse of time via the 'historic' tre
cedar planted in 1734 by the botanist Bernard de
dotted with statues of the personalities who have sl
are statues of Buffon, Lamarck and a rather curio
Daubentin near the labyrinth; while just outside th
rue Linné and rue Cuvier, is the magnificent Cuv

There have been various vineyards in the Jar
centuries, notably under Jean Baptiste Colbert in t
on the hill around what is now the labyrinth. The vi
in the garden's logo, adorning half of its vegetal c

The vin

nted in a flat section of the park in the ecological
on of vines on the rue Geoffroy-St-Hilaire side of
hadowed by buildings and the surrounding trees
acing, received very little sunlight.

n the Ecological Garden of the Jardin des Plantes
esenting the 3 main grape varieties (Gamay,
 Noir) that were traditionally most commonly
ance. There are also a few French/American
ross between Folle Blanche and Noah designed to
nted widely in Gascony for brandy production -
as well as Noah, derived from the Vitis Labrusca
tely cold-resistant varietal, Noah is used in wine
 for Uhudler (an Austrian wine) and Fragolino (a
e).

ardener responsible for the vineyard, reminds us
-de-France (the Paris region) was among the most
s of France. The objective here is not to produce
mbiotic relationships between the vines and the
r this reason, all 'foreign' plants are allowed to
nd the soil is worked superficially by mowing the
ng between the rows. Insects are encouraged since
les in the health of the vines while others serve to
 harm. There are also a few wild vines that have
o the neighbouring trees, which have now reached
s, reminding us that grape vines are creepers and
n-checked, will grow to amazing lengths.

Saint Germain-des-Prés (Paris' smallest vi
3 Place Saint-Germain des Prés, 75006 (Acce.
Saint Germain side in the Square Félix Desr

A small village nestled around the abbey of Sain
consecrated in 558 by the bishop of Paris. In the M
the Philippe Auguste wall and so quite an independ
only to the Pope. The town of Saint-Germain wa
century and had about 600 inhabitants. Among the
it possessed was the 'Clos de Laas', which extend
the rue de la Huchette to the College Mazarin, b
what is now the rue Saint André des Arts.

The Square Félix Desruelles boasts Paris' sma
ten vines of Gamay from the Beaujolais village of
called a vineyard at all. Julienas is one of the ten
and lively wines come from a black Gamay with w
picked. It has good body and when grown natura
can be kept from 5 to 8 years. But the modesty
than compensated by the enthusiasm of its suppor
vines made to the history of Saint-Germain-des-P
in 2007 of the 'St Julienas des Prés' enclosure is
son of Georges Simenon, the popular French auth
featuring the inimitable inspector Maigret. Yves C
French chefs at the origin of 'bistronomy' is also a

The large Abbeys of Saint-Germain-des-Prés, Sai
de Paris, possessed extensive vineyards situated on
hills of Montmorency, Cormeilles en Parisis, Argent
well as other communes. The vines of the plots of I
Châtillon and Fontenay were under the jurisdiction
Prés right up until the Revolution. Other vineyard
included Palaiseau, Celle (Yvelines), Antoni-Verriè
Celle (Saint Cloud), Jouy-en-Josas, Vitry (Val de),
Thiais, Esmans, Massy, Combs (la-Ville), Siccevall
Mesnil (le), Mittainville, Nogent l'Artaud, Mantes,
and Villamilt 'Villamilie Gamo'.

Lands south of the Abbaye extending as far
Montereau also belonged to Saint-Germain-des-P
richest institutions of its time. According to Etien
Pays du Vin (1998), the Abbaye Saint-Germain-de

10,000 'muids' (about 280 litres per muid, therefore a total of 2,800,000 litres) of wine per year from all its holdings. Lafourcade estimates their annual consumption at around 2000 'muids (560,000 litres – enough to provide 500+ monks, nuns and acolytes with 3 litres of wine each, per day), which left them with an astounding 2,240,000 litres to sell.

Wine was thus the principal product for trade and, as mentioned earlier, the economic driver of the Middle Ages. Lafourcade continues: "the quantity of bovines, pigs, sheep and poultry was equally enormous, making wheat

Church of Saint-Germain-des-Prés

seem nothing but a complement. Wine and meat constituted the axis of the Parisian agro-economy."[2] And this was the case for all the great religious orders of the time, not just Saint-Germain-des-Prés. The visible wealth this generated was staggering, creating jealousies and eventually leading to insurrection, the French Revolution being the culmination.

Saint-Germain-des-Prés - Paris' smallest vineyard

2   Lafourcade, Etienne, Paris pays de vin, Presses de Valmy, Paris 1998 - p. 145

Luxembourg Gardens (south-west corner)
Rue Auguste Comte, 75006

In the south-west corner of the Jardin du Luxembourg is the fruit garden. According to the 1809 catalogue of the École Impériale du Luxembourg assembled by Michel Christophe Hervy, who archived the hundreds of fruit species and varieties planted here (Hervy directed the nursery for 46 years and was primarily an arborist), there were no less than 135 red grape varietals and 36 white varietals.

Hervy's contemporary, Jean-Antoine Chaptal (the inventor of 'chaptalisation' – the addition of sugar to the must during fermentation to raise alcohol levels), also wanted to assemble all the species and varieties of vines cultivated in France to create a nomenclature of the different grapes that were known. To develop this project, he had all the Prefects of France collect samples of the existing vines from each department. This is how the greatest collection of vines that existed at the time was created.

By 1842, thanks to the action of Jules-Alexandre Hardy, Gardener-Chef of the Jardin du Luxembourg, the École des Vignes had up to 1,498 different species or varieties and in 1848 this number increased to 1,924.

One of the obscure grape varieties planted in the Luxembourg Gardens

An undated catalogue, attributed to Hardy around the middle of the 19th century and recently found in the Senate archives, accounts for 797 varieties. Unfortunately, this unique ampelographic collection disappeared in the 1860s during work done in this quarter of Paris under the reign of Napoleon III and was never rebuilt.

Today, the collection of vines includes over thirty varieties with obscure names such as 'Cornichon Violette', Foster's White Seedling', 'Perle de Csaea', 'Perlette' and 'Noir Hatif de Marseille'.

The largest collection of grape varietals in the world is still in France though. Not in Paris, but Montpellier and was started 140 years ago. It is now composed of 8,000 accessions from all vine-growing countries.

One of the many grape varietals to be found in the Luxembourg Gardens

Jardin Catherine Labouré
29 Rue de Babylone, 75007

This former vegetable garden takes its name from a young nun who witnessed apparitions of the Virgin in the 19th century, and pilgrims to this day still visit her tomb on the rue du Bac. Originally part of the lands that belong to the Daughters of Charity of Saint Vincent de Paul, it is now leased as a concession to the city of Paris, under whose authority it is maintained. Today, and especially in summer, the garden no longer shelters the Virgin but the many Parisians who come to enjoy a bit of relaxation in the 7,000m² of greenery and lawn. Fruit trees, vine plants, an arbour — the garden has lost nothing of the past.

The vines, which wind themselves around a trellised alleyway extending over 100 metres in length, are Chasselas and Muscat de Hambourg. Planted in 1977 they offer a wonderful shady walk from spring through fall. The grapes are not vinified but are collected to eat.

Vineyard canopy in the Catherine Labouré park

Presbytère de Saint Francois Xavier
12 Place du Président Mithouard, 75007 (Limited public access)

Hidden behind the façade of the Aumonerie across from the imposing church of Saint Francois Xavier at 39 bd des Invalides is an exquisite little garden with trellised vines that were planted around 2005. Though Colette Briot has been looking after the garden for the past 40 years as a volunteer, she was unable to tell us much about the vines since the paper with this information seems to have disappeared. There are only about 8 vines, but they have been trained to grow up the trellis, spreading their branches and leaves over the top to form a canopy. The grapes are not vinified and what is not eaten by birds and insects is picked by Colette as one of the little perks of her volunteering. There is another vine of Chasselas that has been allowed to grow up against a wall on the other side of the park, its leaves and branches winding around other creepers and a very healthy-looking vine of passion fruit. A veritable garden of Eden.

The vine trellis of the Presbytère St-François Xavier

Bistrot Mélac
42 Rue Léon Frot, 75011

The Baco vine that covers the façade of the winebar, which was once the fiefdom of the moustachioed Jacques Mélac, is from his father's vineyard in Corbières. For over 30 years, this colourful personality, who single-handedly personified the spirit of the vine in Paris, hosted a 'vendange' party resembling a village fête.

For several years, he produced a symbolic wine made from these grapes that was called 'Château Charonne'. Only women were invited to pick the grapes and only children allowed to stomp them with their bare feet. The production was very small, around 40 bottles, given away during a raffle attended by locals as well as by visitors from around the world, animated by a personality from the arts. Jacques sold his winebar several years ago, but it has carried on serving wine and the vine continues to flourish.

Baco vine at Bistrot Melac

Jardin Truillot
82 Boulevard Voltaire, 75011

This large green space of almost 5,600 m2 created between Richard-Lenoir and Voltaire boulevards (11th) opened to the public on Monday 16 July 2018 and thus is one of the most recent additions to the city's green spaces that includes vines. The intention from the beginning was part of an initiative for the greening of the quarter, which is one of the poorest neighbourhoods of the city in terms of green spaces.

Designed by landscapers Marie-Odile Ricard and Jean-Marc Le Névanic, it has a beautiful view of the Saint-Ambroise church. It includes a crèche (daycare), two playgrounds in a meadow and a vast lawn bordered by flowering fallows, grape vines, and fruit trees. A shared garden and an educational garden are accessible to residents and schools in the neighbourhood. The garden was barely finished, however, when some already dissatisfied residents

Jardin Truillot vines with Saint-Ambroise in the background

complained, demanding the closure of this green space at night. At this writing, it remains open 24 hours a day and this policy generates nocturnal and sonic noise in this vast environment that resonates, disturbing those trying to sleep.

The final layout of the Truillot garden involved the demolition of the building which housed 'La Grosse Bouteille' bar, located at 64, boulevard Richard Lenoir. This bar took its name from the huge bottle perched on its roof, an old advertisement made famous by Robert Doisneau, who photographed it twice in 1959 and in 1961. The proposal to keep a souvenir of this bottle was accepted, resulting in a phase of consultation that has seemingly ensured the ongoing absence of the bottle in question.

Jardin Truillot vines

Square Léo Ferré
Rue de Cîteaux, 75012

Located in the heart of the Faubourg Saint-Antoine, the Léo-Ferré square was created as part of an urban development operation in 2009. It is named after the French poet and singer/composer whose dynamic and controversial live performances began after the Second World War and continued until his death. His many hit singles include 'Paname', 'La Solitude', 'Avec le temps', 'C'est extra', 'Jolie Môme' and 'Paris canaille'.

Installed on the remains of a factory of craftsmen working with wood and metal, the garden had to respect the spirit of the Faubourg Saint-Antoine. This past inspired the main directions of the project. The expectations and requests of residents were also numerous. It is accessible by the rue de Cîteaux, the passage Brulon, and the impasse Druinot.

Today, this small, long forest garden is bordered by a passage, an historic dead end and some low buildings that bear witness to the Paris of artisans. It is a haven of peace away from the urban bustle, adjoining the shared community garden of the association 'La Commune Libre d'Aligre' created

Square Léo Ferré vines

in March 2004. The children of the nursery of the passage Druinot, the furniture craftsmen of the 'hôtel Artisanal' and the inhabitants of the surrounding social housing are the first to benefit.

The garden is made up of a central alley which winds from the rue de Cîteaux to the impasse Druinot. On each side, mounds of land form valleys punctuated by trees and shrubs of all kinds.

It is also a garden in memory of the wood trades with several installations evoking these trades: pergolas, trees and shrubs, some of which recall the forest settlement on the outskirts of Paris, benches, a pontoon in oak, the wooden cobblestones inserted into the ground in the games area.

Fruit trees and shrubs (blackcurrant, medlar among them) pair with the vegetable garden of the shared garden and initiate the transition with the educational garden. A pergola on a stone wall separates the shared garden from the public garden.

The vines that are planted here are another connection to Paris' vineyard history. Planted to Chasselas like those of the town of Thomery, they are trellised along a wall. The grapes are collected each year by the municipal gardeners or eaten by birds and other local wildlife.

The hidden vineyard of the Square Léo Ferré

Jardin de Reuilly - Paul Pernin
15 Rue Albinoni, 75012

Vines seem to find themselves hidden in plain view in quite a few public gardens and this shady park in between Dugommier and Montgallet Metro stations is no exception. Asking various people (including a gardener who works there) if they knew where the vines were, no one was able to guide us, so we simply wandered about until we found them. This is perhaps quite normal given that most urban dwellers would be quite incapable of identifying anything other than the most common plants. Winding their way up and over an arbour in the south-east corner of the park, there are several vines, possibly Chasselas, planted here sometime in the past 25 years and are fundamentally a kind of ornamentation that provides cooling shade in hot weather.

Park Paul Pernin vines

Le Clos Reuilly, 75012

Private, inaccessible and hidden, this is one of the most astounding collections of vines that have been given free expression to grow naturally. The branches stretching up from the four massive Baco vines cover several hundred square metres and their trunks are like trees. The vines are, alas, the exclusive delight of the inhabitants of this confidential courtyard in Paris' 12th arrondissement. The shade the vines provide has been extremely welcome during the dog days of August, maintaining a temperature in the mid 20s when it's 30 or more outside. The Clos Reuilly hasn't made wine recently because Angélique, the proprietor and former winemaker, has been waiting for the new generation to take over. In the meantime, the grapes are being eaten by birds who choose the ripest among the bunches, leaving them with the appearance of being well spaced.

Grape vine planted in 1950

In 1970, Angélique, her husband, one of her brothers, and a cousin settled in the alley (they own the three ground floor flats) and decided to take over the maintenance of the vine arbours planted between 1950 and 1955 by the former owners. Every year the arbours are pruned by professionals with the objective of making them more beautiful. Speaking of the district's winegrowing past, she relates that there was once a convent where the mother abbots had, as in all abbeys, their own vegetable garden and vineyard. Reuilly, like so many other quarters of Paris, has a long viticultural history and these vines are a living testimony to an ongoing tradition of wine making.

Clos Reuilly courtyard

La Commanderie du Clos
9bis Rue Norvins, 75018

The headquarters of the Commanderie du Clos on the rue Norvins in Montmartre are surrounded by vines planted to Pinot Noir, which, like the Clos Montmartre, are also used to make wine. The building is unique in shape as it was once a water tower that would regularly be filled from the Seine by the local fire brigade for grey water uses such as watering gardens or putting out fires. Today, the tower serves as a place for hosting the meetings of the 'commanderie', for cultural and artistic events and for wine tastings.

The wine of Montmartre lacked a vinous brotherhood to praise its qualities both in France and around the world and so in 1983, Maurice His — President of the Republic of Montmartre — supported by several

La Commanderie du Clos garden with vines

wine lovers, created the only wine brotherhood in Paris. The companions' ceremonial dress is wine red embellished with gold and silver. Maurice His, succeeded Robert Rivière, who headed the 'P'tits Poulbots' (a dispensary on the rue Lepic that was set up to help the poor children of Montmartre). Alain Valentin, the current Grand Master reigns over this Montmartrois institution, which has become a sanctum of tradition and an ambassador for the traditions that typify Montmartre.

Members of the Commanderie du Clos

Square Suzanne Buisson
7 bis Rue Girardon, 75018

The long vine suspended above the entrance to this little square on the rue Girardot is only metres away from the Château des Brouillards, the location of the last vineyard of Montmartre prior to the plantation of the 'Clos Montmartre' in 1934.

In addition to the lush foliage of the vine (that again reminds us of the true nature of the vine as a creeper, extending its tendrils and branches out laterally over several metres) this green space is decorated with a statue of Saint Denis, the first bishop of Paris, beheaded and carrying his head in his hands. The statue marks the passage of Denis who, tortured in the 3rd century by the Romans and in the company of the priest Rustique and the archdeacon Éleuthère, purportedly walked carrying his head to the place of his burial, the current city of Saint-Denis, stopping at a fountain at Mont Martyrium (Montmartre) to wash his head. According to Hilduin de Saint-Denis, this mythological source is located on the plot where the Château des Brouillards was built.

The robust vine above the entrance to the Square Suzanne Buisson

Square Nadar
2 Rue Saint-Éleuthère, 75018

Named for the Lyonnais Félix Tournachon, known as Nadar (1820-1910), this small square below Sacre Coeur has terraced vines planted to table grapes that are eaten by the park's gardeners or by the birds. Given their location, the vines are most certainly planted on soil that once hosted the 'Haut-Coteau' vineyard belonging to the Abbaye de Montmartre.

Nadar made his fame as a great photographer. After coming to Paris to study medicine, he quickly abandoned his books to devote himself to writing (and in 1849 founded the 'Revue Comique') and, subsequently, the relatively new art of photography. He met with success thanks to personalities like Georges Sand and Théophile Gautier, whose photographic portraits he made. He also took the first aerial photographs using hot-air balloons (1858).

A wall marks the presence of the Montmartre reservoirs, which were built in 1889 in the Byzantine style of the Sacre Coeur: its corner turrets pierced with loopholes are reminiscent of a fortress and its 5 basins have a capacity of 11,000 m3.

Square Nadar vines

Located between rue Azaïs and rue Saint-Éleuthère below the Sacre Coeur Basilica is a statue built in homage to the Chevalier de la Barre (born in 1745), who was beheaded and burned in 1766 because he was suspected of having desecrated two crucifixes and of having blasphemed.

Sacre Coeur

Eglise Saint Serge
93 rue de la Crimée 75019

This is not a vineyard, but a single vine planted in 1935, which has the distinction of being the longest vine in Paris (47 metres in one direction and 17 metres in the other, measured in 2019), another reminder that vines are creepers and when left to their own devices, will grow to extraordinary lengths.

The grape varietal is a hybrid called Verdelet created by Albert Seibel and Georges Couderc who were both from the Ardéche region. Pairing European 'vitis vinifera' with phylloxera resistant American rootstocks, they sought to create hybrids that were resistant to this insect that devastated vines in the late 19th century. The history of this vine was also at the centre of a polemic around the use of hybrids that pitted 'chemists' against 'Americanists' in the struggle to find a cure for the ravages of phylloxera.

Seibel died in 1936 and since then the hybrids have generally fallen out of favour, branded as producing mediocre wines by the French authorities. But the Verdelet vine on the rue Crimée lives on, blissfully unaware of the arguments that once raged around it.

The longest vine in Paris

La Musée du Vin
5 Sq. Charles Dickens, 75016

Located in a former quarry that supplied stone for the construction of buildings between the 13th and 18th centuries, it was also used by the Brothers of the Ordre des Minimes of the Passy Convent to store their wine in the 16th and 17th centuries. The museum today has a permanent collection of more than 2,000 objects that "pay tribute to all those who have worked to produce world-famous wines". In addition to the museum, there is a tasting room with classes in tasting and a restaurant that offers traditional French cuisine.

Museé du Vin

A few isolated, random vines.

The creeping tendrils of vines have attached themselves to every quarter of the city, their sun-reaching branches gently swaying in parks and gardens, in courtyards, and climbing up walls, luxuriant foliage softening the hard edges of the cityscape.

Quai de la Mégisserie, 75001

The vines planted in pots along the wall of this quai by the Seine have been trained to climb the wall and in only five years have grown several metres. They are another example of the will to 'vegetalise' the city with vines playing a prominent role in the process.

Quai de la Mégisserie

Quai de la Hôtel de Ville, 75004

There is a beautiful arched vine trellis in the Jardin des Arts Albert Schweizer at the corner of the Quai de l'Hôtel de Ville and the rue des Nonnains d'Hyeres, across from the Hôtel de Sens. Its thick trunk suggests it was planted at least 30 years ago and is an eloquent display of the vine's capacity to ornament and provide shade.

Jardin des Arts Albert Schweizer

Rue Cuvier, Rue Jussieu, Rue Guy de la Brosse 75005

The rue Cuvier, which runs between the Jardin des Plantes and Jussieu has a 'rogue' vine that may well be a vestige of the days of the Halle aux Vins, which was originally situated on this land. There were undoubtedly vines growing among the warehouses and it's easy to imagine this vine as a carry-over of that period, with another at 17 rue Jussieu. There is also an exuberant, well-established vine among the superabundant verdure at 14 rue Cuvier, and another hidden in the back courtyard of 13 rue Guy de la Brosse.

A living souvenir of the Halle aux Vins

Rue Geoffroy Saint-Hilaire, 75005 (the Mosque)

Inside the tea garden of the Mosque (entrance at the corner of Geoffroy Saint-Hilaire and the rue Daubenton) as far in as you can go and then up a set of stairs on the right, there is a profuse vine that has thread its tendrils over a lattice work, providing shade for the tea drinkers below.

The vine shading the roof of the Mosque tea house

Rue Mouffetard, 75005

Historic rue Mouffetard is known for its open market and as a landmark of 'old Paris'. The street is part of the hillsides of the Montagne Saint Geneviève, which was covered in vines in all directions through till the 18th century and undoubtedly planted by the Romans. The vines that are growing along the wall of the municipal kindergarten on the corner of Mouffetard and the rue Saint Médard are another vestige of the vine's presence in this oldest of Paris neighbourhoods.

Vigorous vines on the rue Mouffetard

Rue Cardinal Lemoine, 75005

At 47 rue Cardinal Lemoine, on the left side of the courtyard of the Hotel le Brun (built in 1700, the painter Watteau lived here, as did the Comte de Buffon), there is a profusion of greenery, among which a grape vine triumphs in height and vigour.

Exuberant vine tendrils on the rue Cardinal Lemoine

Medieval Garden, 2 rue de Cluny, 75005

Sprawling, unkempt vines can be found in the walled section of the medieval garden of the Cluny Museum. To see them, you need to enter the garden off the Blvd Saint-Germain and then peer through the lattice work of the wooden enclosure. The current garden is based on medieval documents but is above all a contemporary creation, even if it is medieval in inspiration.

The sprawling vines of the Cluny Garden on blvd Saint-Germain

Rue Pierre Semard, 75009

Near the bottom of the rue Semmard is a wall with vines planted in holes in the pavement that have allowed them to penetrate the soil and bring forth an abundance of branches, leaves and grapes. Their verdant foliage and decorative aspect, like all vines, disappears in winter when all that remains are bare branches and gnarly rootstock. This is another exuberant example of the vine's presence in the urban landscape.

Vines covering a wall on the rue Pierre Semard

Rue Servan and rue Duranti, 75011

The profusion of vine leaves cascading over the wall of the Servan Elementary School at the corner of Rue Servan and rue Duranti has a history that seems to have been forgotten. Like many of the vines that continue to grow in unexpected places, whoever was there when they were planted can no longer be found. Those who live with them daily take them for granted and, as they would for other flora, rarely question their origins. So, we are unable to name the varietal that is growing here, though an obvious guess would be Chasselas given its location directly next to the wall that surrounds the playground and so reminiscent of the vines of Thomery.

Vine covered wall rue Servan and rue Duranti

Villa Auguste Blanqui, 75013

Hidden in gardens, behind walls and at times trailing over the façade of houses, there are also grape vines adorning private residences. This is the case here on this little street in the 13th arrondissement of Paris, where the residents benefit from the perennial tenacity of the vine as it stretches out in all directions along the street. The most noticeable vines here extend over the façade of a building reaching out in both directions over several metres and every year, the street is associated with the events of the 'Fête de la Vigne' and the movement to 'vegetalise Paris'.

Villa Auguste Blanqui vines

Village house, 3 rue la Vieuville, 75018

Like the reference above, the facade of the house at the corner of the Rue la Vieuville across from the park with the *Mur des Je t'Aime* (the wall of I love you's) by the Place des Abbesses is covered with a well-established vine that adds to the impression that so many corners of Montmartre give of being in the country. This street marks the location of the former Abbey de Montmartre, and was originally called the rue de la Mairie, the street of the town hall, where Georges Clemenceau presided as mayor and the poet Paul Verlaine was married.

Vine covered village house in Montmartre.

Afterword

Exploring the vineyards of Paris and hosting people from around the world on '*Paris Wine Walks*' (www.paris-wine-walks.com) has been an ongoing education and one of the best ways to discover the history of the city's arrondissements. The vine lives on and its presence is a reassuring confirmation that civilisation, nowhere more eloquently reflected than in the cultivation of the vine and the production of wine, is still a possibility.

The renaissance that is taking place in viticulture around the Ile de France is a further testimony to this possibility and will be the subject of my next book.

Wine is an ancient soul that has been around for thousands of years. When we hold a glass of wine up to the light, we are peering into the essence of a living organism symbolic of our relationship to nature. It is often described as a gift of the gods and its capacity to inebriate inspires lofty thoughts and deep reflection.

Wine brings together the best of human artistry and makes philosophers of farmers. When I'm on the road exploring vineyards, every visit is a discovery, or a re-discovery, and every vineyard is unique and distinctive. There is no drink that is more complex than wine and its stories are endless.

As Colette wrote, "The vine and wine are great mysteries. In the plant kingdom, the vine alone is capable of rendering intelligible the taste of the earth. What faithfulness in the translation! It feels and expresses the secrets of the soil through the grape. With flint, we sense it is alive, melding, nourishing, and arid chalk cries tears of gold through wine."[3]

This book is dedicated to all of those around the world who plant, tend and cultivate the vine, celebrating its fruit through vinification as well as to all of those who enjoy their labours and strive to learn more about wine's mysteries. Santé!

3   Sidonie Gabrielle Colette (Prisons et Paradis, 1932)

Bibliography & References

Le vin au Moyen Age, Tour Jean Sans Peur, Paris 2012

The Goodman of Paris (translation Eileen Power), The Boydell Press, Woodbridge Suffolk, 2006

Boiron, Christine — Les Vins de Paris, Glénat, Grenoble 1988

Brook, Stephen — A Century of Wine, Mitchell Beazley, 2000

Classen, Albercht — The Poems of Oswald Von Wolkenstein, Palgrave Macmillan, Camden 2008

Duby, Georges — The Age of the Cathedrals, University of Chicago Press, Chicago 1981

Duby, Georges — Le Moyen Age, 987-1460, Hachette, Paris 1987

Galet, Pierre — Dictionnaire Encyclopédique des Cépages, Libre & Solidaire, Paris 2018

Hillairet, Jacques — Dictionnaire Historique des rues de Paris, Les Editions de Minuit, Paris 1963

Jacquelin, Louis et Poulain, René — Vignes et Vins de France, Flammarion, Paris 1960

James, John — The Travellers Key to Medieval France, Alfred A. Knopf, New York 1986

Lachiver, Marcel — Vin, Vigne et Vignerons en region Parisienne du XVII au XIX siècle, Société Historique et Archaeologique de Pontoise, du Val d'Oise et du Vexin, Pontoise 1982

Lafoucade, Etienne — Paris pays du vin, Presses de Valmy, Paris 1998

Lagarce, Stéphane — Le Grand Précis des Vins au Naturel, Editions Homo Habilis, Vitry-sur-Seine

Lopez, Robert S. — The Commercial Revolution of the Middle Ages, 950-1350, Cambridge University Press, Cambridge 2005

McGovern, Patrick E — Uncorking the Past, University of California Press, Berkley CA, 2009

McGovern, Patrick E — Ancient Wine, Princeton University Press, Princeton NJ, 2007

de Montmollin, Francoise — Un Repas Historique Moyen Age, Editions Ouest France, Lille 2015

Mouraux, Lionel — Bercy au fil du Temps, Le Point, Paris 2004

Ollivier, Claude — La Vigne, Les Croqueurs de Pommes, Troyes 2012

Passot, Pierre — Montmartre Forever, Editions Artena, Paris 2010

Phillips, Rod — French Wine, a history, University of California Press, Oakland CA, 2016

Ragache, Gilles — Vignobles d'Île-de-France, Les Presses du Village, Etrepilly 2005

Robinson, Jancis — Vines, Grapes and Wines, Mitchell Beazley, London 1994

Rose, Susan — The Wine Trade in Medieval Europe 1000-1500, Bloomsbury, London 2015

Roux, Simone — Paris in the Middle Ages, University of Pennsylvania Press, 2003

Oakland CA, 2016

Ragache, Gilles — Vignobles d'Île-de-France, Les Presses du Village, Etrepilly 2005

Robinson, Jancis — Vines, Grapes and Wines, Mitchell Beazley, London 1994

Rose, Susan — The Wine Trade in Medieval Europe 1000-1500, Bloomsbury, London 2015

Roux, Simone — Paris in the Middle Ages, University of Pennsylvania Press, 2003

Acknowledgements

There have been many people who have contributed to the writing of this book in one way or another and I apologise in advance if I have forgotten anyone.

I would particularly like to thank Dr. James Bugslag for his attentive reading of the early draughts and his comments and corrections regarding life in the Middle Ages; Charlotte Mosely for her astute comments and suggestions; Patrice Bersac for his vast knowledge of the wines of the Île-de-France and role in their current renaissance; Hamish Cameron for his exceedingly generous editorial interventions; the Mooney family for their spirit; Anna Bonde for her 'cabanon' in the Luberon; Simon and Olivia for the use of their house in Burgundy and Glenn Burney for making the arrangements; the Eonnet family for their 5-star tent in Normandy; the Stirling brothers and friends for their zeal; Caroline Petit for extensive corrections and suggestions; Jody Jenkins and Pierre Mackenzie for kindly proofing and commenting on an early draught; the Cave de Belleville, L'Etiquette, Magnum, Lot of Wine, la Cave à Michel, La Chambre Noir, Bon Vivant, Devine, Gargantua, Vignes (Le Canon d'Achille), Le Ballon Rouge, Le Petit Atelier Ramay, Chez Eugène, la Pointe du Grouin, Bacchus et Ariane, La Cremerie, le Comptoir du Marché, Freddy's, Caluche, Café de la Nouvelle Mairie and Les Pipos for hosting *Paris Wine Walks* and introducing me to new wines; Katherine for her editorial and photo savvy and for really being there, and lastly, my daughter Chloé for her curiosity, enthusiasm, accompaniment, wine appreciation, love and support.

Although the greatest care has been taken to check sources and the information included herein, the author assumes full responsibility for any possible inaccuracies.

BOARD AND BENCH
—— PUBLISHING ——

Find this and all Board + Bench Ebooks at
www.imbiblioapp.com

WWW.BOARDANDBENCH.COM
WWW.IMBIBLIOAPP.COM

**Best Drinks Culture App
Gourmand Awards**